EXILES AND PLEASURES:
TAUNGGYI DREAMING

poems by

Jaspal Kaur Singh

Finishing Line Press
Georgetown, Kentucky

EXILES AND PLEASURES:
TAUNGGYI DREAMING

Copyright © 2023 by Jaspal Kaur Singh
ISBN 979-8-88838-028-4 First Edition
All rights reserved under International and Pan-American Copyright Conventions. No part of this book may be reproduced in any manner whatsoever without written permission from the publisher, except in the case of brief quotations embodied in critical articles and reviews.

Publisher: Leah Huete de Maines
Editor: Christen Kincaid
Cover Art: Uzma Ahmad
Author Photo: Kym Ghee
Cover Design: Elizabeth Maines McCleavy and Shravan Rajagopal

Order online: www.finishinglinepress.com
also available on amazon.com

Author inquiries and mail orders:
Finishing Line Press
P. O. Box 1626
Georgetown, Kentucky 40324
U. S. A.

Table of Contents

I. migrants and immigrations: generations and interconnectedness

a monkey riding on mother's back 1
Interconnected: You and I 5
Her Uncle 6
In the land of the greenghosts 7
Black Foreigners in Burma 8
My father's brother, you *arse*! 9
Whispering Pine of Taunggyi Mountains 10
Ma: Punjaban 11
Chawla Sisters: Before the Dispersal 12
Diasporic Peregrinations 13
Banyan Tree Ghost 14
Moonless Burmese Night 15
Bollywood: Shammi Kapoor in Taunggyi 16
Shan Mountains: Before the Massacre 17
Piquant and Tart: Girlhood 18
Dusk in the mountains of Shan States 19
Monks in Saffron Robes: Part One 20
Destinies 21

2. exiles and dislocations: love, marriage and family

You and I: Interconnected beyond the Mountains 25
Motherland 26
Delhi Girl 27
Roots of Love and Barks of Desire 28
Lost in Taunggyi 32
Wings of Hintha 33
An offshoot of the tree 34
Swirling 35
New Arrivals: New Delhi 36
What is love, Ma? 37
You Talk Too Much 38

Border Wounds...39
Bina (named after a star) 40
Liar: Two Raindrops...41
Krishna: The God of Love 42
Home..43
Famine & Plentitude 44
Ganga Ghats..46
Border Wars and Enlightened Love 47

3. diasporic peregrinations: myriads encounters

Gray Ocean Pearl..51
Vasco da Gama: Oil Lamps and Stars 52
Kynsna..53
Uluru-Kaja Tjuta National Park, Central Australia: Mother
     and Child..54
Between Zambia and Zimbabwe..56
Cynthia, a Maid in South African 57
Kars: Pale Moon in Thunder 58
Halong Bay 59
They call them *Paisa, Chavanni, Athani*..60
Ocean of no return 61
Learning to sing like never before..63
In Search of Nothingness 64
Fuchsia Tea..65
Oregon's Crater Lake...66
Walking in Two Worlds...67
Raat Ki Rani 68
A Coiled Serpent Speaks 69
Ripples..70
Counting Blessing: 71
Appeasing the Goddess 72
A Riddle for You 73
Time signature..74

4. into the sunset: or, circling back

Immigrant 77
Moonlit Nights 78
A Dark Grain of Sand 79
Emptiness 80
Plentitude 81
Healer 82
Turtle, Turtle in the Sea 83
Weathering It 84
Dance like Rumi 85
Military coup in Burma: Again 87
Rebirth (After Ada Limón's "Before") 88
Moonlit Superior Shores to the Cascades: A Journey Continues 89
The Haunting 90
Civilizing Mission (After Norman Dubie's "The Kingdom") 91
Chakwal: Great-Grandmother's Ancestral Village 92
The Wisest One (After Naomi Shibab Nye's "What Kind of Fool
    Am I?") 93
Dislocated: Down the Rabbit Hole 94
On Gratification (After Traci Brimhall's "Dear Thanatos") 95
Drawing Circles and Lines 96
No longer fragmented 97
Home for *Echakway* 98
Homes and Hearts: I have left behind 99
Climbing Malibu Creek Canyon 102
Monks in Saffron Robes: Part Two 103
Home is the Diasporic 104

Acknowledgments 107

*I dedicate this book to my late grandmothers, Laaj Kaur and Bishan Kaur,
my mother, Tej Kaur, my father, Prab Joth Singh,
my sisters, Satwant Singh and the late Bina Singh,
my daughter, Gitanjali Kaur Singh, my son, Gautam Mohan Singh,
and my granddaughter, Karina Singh Cho.*

1. migrants and immigrations: generations and interconnectedness

a monkey riding on mother's back

having learnt to swim, breathe,
almost fly in atmospheres green, rare,
with animists, earthworshippers
and *nats:*

a baby monkey
riding on her mother's back
in Big Mountains
swings from tree to tree

reading ancient texts
in *Gurudwara* about warrior gurus
and saints, father, laughing at
pakhandis, hypocrites, who
hate Hindus, Muslims, Dalits,

but say *Waheguru* on each breath,
broken promises and bones, crowing
in bruised bodies buried in shallow graves.

i roll *rotis* with mother in early morning,
we women and girls sit tight

>by blackened iron griddle with log fires,
>underneath: it glows with embers
>as brothers knead dough and cut potatoes
>for the *langar* in communal kitchen

spiced *dal* and cauliflowers
shared among the faithful
in dreamy Shan life,

but suddenly, the Valleys fill
with change, khaki uniforms,
combat boots and "Ne Win
Sten" TZ 45 submachine guns

>*hope lies like a snowflake on lashes*

> *hope lies like dreams on silver leaves*
> > *hope lies like sleeping children on mountaintops*
> > > *hope crumbles like the moon in crater lake*

who among us will dwell with strangers
when love leaves you with a mouthful
of memories like the aftertaste of crushed cardamoms
in hot tea made with goat's milk and honey—

> what other taste do you crave?
> cradling lives in fearful arms
> like lambs before Ramadan
> stealing them away to safety

in far lands of monochromatic shades
feeding them ambrosia and blood
of ones lost before to dreams deferred
and, climbing on crushed skulls,

> slip on way to the top: a crystal light
> shatters and shards stab the retina
> in land of lost opportunities,

> love gone, lovers left, lives searching
> for more, as if enough is never enough—
> my soul, holding your thoughts, spill:

> waking up not to remember the greenland
> dream of childhood when I crouched by

father's feet, as he bowed to the *Granth*
face alight with love and paternal pride
when I touched mother's small hands
carrying female ancestors' stories

> like secrets in scarred wombs
> to nights when I wake to blood
> stains from splintered thoughts
> transform to wisdom for descendants

    as if an overflowing heart freezes
      as if a body's touch deadens
        as if lostness is a desired space
          as if refracted ideas of strangers are one's own

watered by the collected beads
and pearls from the memory land
i never knew hope was a creature
who desired sacrifice,

    as if hungry for your unborn children,
      as if lonely for your home in the lost land
        as if walking on thorns to find love
          as if children entombed alive in walls for religion

as if fractured skulls and grilled flesh
  of worshippers, pinched by hot pincers,
    as if stumbling footsteps over rough terrains
      scattered with torn limbs on way to ancestral lands

  as if destiny was not a place
    but an in-between space forever alien,
      not yet home and no longer safe,

      the estranged monkey, bereft of mother,
        is rife with yearning for belonging,

there, the body skims like ants on surfacewater
not yet drowned, but just with feet in,
frantic, naked mother with crooked bones,
white hair to back of knees, as fantasized

  in stories of Punjab, turns her back
  as arrows puncture & taking spilled guts
  in earthenware pot—the baby monkey
  returns to sit by the largest lake in Asia, Inlay,

        envisioning tadpoles and mangoes

in buckets of cool rain drops
collected from corrugated tin roofs
in the land of the greenghosts.

Interconnected: You and I

You were there: when I needed a tiny helping hand. You recognized me from before, lifetimes ago when we were playmates, helping each other cross streams, climbing Shan mountains, relishing Rangoon heat. In flavors of mangoes, papayas, rambutans and mangosteens. In swaying palms and bamboos of the tropics and in Punjabi fields. You sang and danced for the simple joy of a farmer's life—fecund *and* ever-present.

Her Uncle

Her uncle recites Byron in perfect
        English as he hikes with her

on Shan hills. A small dark girl with long
        braids, deep eyes, delights in orchids.

Shan girls walk by envying
        the camaraderie of such handsome

shadowed people, black Indians, *kala mai*.
        Smelling of coconut and mustard oil.

He feeds her purpleskinned mangosteen,
        touches her tender breasts.

For days, she smells of *pin sain di,*
        crab apples left to dry on the tin roof.

They use them in spiced curry
        to add tartness to the fragrance.

in the land of the greenghosts

where, during a late summer evening bath
with water kept in blue & yellow iron drums,
two brownskinned darkeyed indian girls
splash each other, touch hands bodies
when a sudden cold breeze blows
a fiery red hanuman-shaped balloon
over the frolicking girls, Radha and Sita:

Love is a story told by grandmother.

Black Foreigners in Burma

- I am a black indian

- *kula mai*

- *kula chi*

- *kula sau*

- *kula* smell

- butter

- ghee

- spices

- ma's armpits

- grandma's pillows

&, as a child, I remember the smell of Indian ghee, the sting of spices, the feel of ma's armpits, grandmother's breasts, havens I withdrew to so I could become invisible.

My father's brother, you *arse!*

Chacha, you used to beat us children with a tennis racquet.

You used your leather sandals as whips on our bodies.

You threatened chili powder on our tongues you called sly.

Once, my father's pet monkey

      ran off. It whooped at me. I threw a pebble at it.   she grabbed

  my hair and   shook me.   tore my book.   bit my thigh.

you sneered at father:

You can't even be bothered to buy bananas to feed your own children; is she your daughter?

      Ridiculed, father took me to the doctor for a shot.

That evening, they took his pet monkey away from him.

          And   the monkey and   you   screeched.

Whispering Pine of Taunggyi Mountains

There's no plant that gives more shade than a mother's love,
& so unlike others, it dies when its flowers wilt.
    So say Indian poets and sages.

In the outdoor bath in cold weather,
   tubs of water—a mountain full of gray uniformed enemies
        to demolish.

A thick wooden stick to beat dirt out of clothes,
  Ma, you show me tricks for beautification,
    a dry cloth rubbed against wet foot,
     dead skin and soiled worms
crawling up my legs. I squash them dead.

Frigid sunny mornings to wash uncut Sikh hair,
drums of water—warming in sun.
    You chase me, leather shoe raised,
     my long hair streaming down the back,

       hating cool water, mountain climate.

Breaking a twig from neem tree,

     your small frame a soldier,
       you bring it down hard on tender shoulders,

  dirty demon! Clean yourself!

  and I, at first struggling like a wild Burmese tiger caught in net,

am suddenly appeased as you gently wash my long hair
with soaked *reetha* seeds and *kimundi* barks.

You smear crushed dried orange peels mixed in yogurt
on my skinny body and angular face.

You pour buckets of sun-soaked water to rejuvenate.
Now, skinny one, your skin and face will glow.

Ma: Punjaban

you told stories of Sikh women
writer warriors, mold breakers
yet, Ma, you died quietly
I resented eulogies by those

who did not know You.
They say, *Ma, full of grace*
she knew her place
praised her deeds

service to others, her creed
she died taking care of her man
a self-sacrificing wo-man
but, Ma, I remember

your tender oval face becoming
square jawed with suppressed rage
as grandmother disparaged your caste
of tailors from Amritsar

like steel wool, you cut.
In face of Burmese army aggression
frail in body but not in spirit
you carried family from country

to inhospitable country.
travelled days in dirty trains
worked the in-between terrains
in Imphal, Moreh, borders of no man's

land between India and Burma
makeshift huts and unknown geography
to feed your college-going daughters and sons.
You balanced your fragmented self.

Punjaban Sherni, a Buddhist, a monk.
why, mother, did you not fight for your own life?
    You love like silver-leaf bells on Shan Pagodas,
      earthenware diya lamps in the District of Chakwal.

Chawla Sisters: Before the Dispersal

older sisters call me scarecrow.

           mother, you massage our faces,

    necks and arms in mustard oil,

              a little cream mixed

with powdered chickpeas.

           Indian smell!

we wear our little *lungies*

      tied around our budding breasts,

           pointed nipples with hard coins inside

      second sister pour buckets of water on my head body

we dry our luscious uncut hair in the sun

      you massage coconut oil, comb and braid long hair

           with colorful homemade *parandi* tasseled with tiny bells.

Diasporic Peregrinations

Mother, you are: sniff kisses Burmese style,
wings wisp on parched summer days,
wet bodies in stormy monsoon rains,
papayas, mangosteens, pineapples,
sucking rain-cooled mango flesh,
licking pit for last bit of juice.

You are: spicy coconut noodles and fermented
tea salad. Pungent, with garlic and ginger—
          like intoxicated bridal drums, dancing, clapping,
          of Punjabans' hands—
click of spoon on *dholak*.

Rhythmic *boliyans* at weddings.
Pomegranate chutney with hot chilies on grinding stones.
Phulkas on hot embers puffed and crisp.
Homemade *lassi*—in clay pot placed between your feet
& a rope twined between your fingers, churning.

You love like hymns in the Himalayas,
          Soft *kirtan* in early Amritsar dawn.

Banyan Tree Ghost

Maung Maung. Tin Tin.
Surjit. Pal. Bina.
Daljit. Sato. Khin Ma La.

        Moonlit tropical nights
           we play children's games.

Htaut See.
                Catch and run.
Lime lines on dirt ground.
        One side, four.
          Other side, four.
                  Can you run?

Play Nyaung Pin Tasey.
        Come and catch me, Banyan Ghost.
                If you can.

What do you eat, *Tasey?*
        Banyan fruit.
Where do you live, *Tasey?*
                Banyan branch.

When you die, who will you scare, *Tasey?*
                You! *Ahh Ma Leh!*
I plead, voice trembling.
            What will you eat, ghost?

        I. am. coming.
        to. catch. you.

Winds blow on tall teaks.
            He comes.
        Every night.
Banyan Tree Ghost
            in Burma.

Moonless Burmese Night

I am afraid of nightly darkness, knocks on doors.
I am alarmed at bright and brown uniforms—
BSI, Bureau of Special Investigation.
Rifles in hands, their round eyes probe.
So, trembling, we wake—I clutch ma's tiny hands.
From behind her, I peek, feeling her tremble.
They touched the beds and sheets. I see my father.
His long hair, long beard. Coverless. Turbanless.
He is shamed. They touched our drawers. They tossed our clothes.
They say they look for contraband goods but take our dreams instead.

Penniless, we left the country,
our home lost into a   fragmenting   mist.

Bollywood: Shammi Kapoor in Taunggyi

So young, like Presley, you writhe and sing
Western-style songs and my 13-year-old heart fills

with dreams of India, oh! To pick fresh apples
in trees of Kashmir! Ride a convertible

and sing a song of love or perch atop a cart
in fields of sugar cane or in tea gardens

with lovely girls in colorful *ghaghra choli*
dancing along with you in perfect rhythm

your reddish lips and blue eyes, as
you sing, *meyri jaan wah wah wah!*

meri jaan wah wah wah wah wah!

You, son of fair-skinned and blue-eyed clan
from north. You sing a song

for damsel in distress barely a few
years older than me: O, sing a *junglee* song!

Chahey koi mujhe junglee kahey!

       I don't care if anyone calls me a savage!

Shan Mountains: Before the Massacre

The bazaar fills with Pa Oh mountain people,
dark blue garments, purple embroidery,
redblue rags spread on dirt floor,
        ripe mangoes, papayas, corn.

The tranquil and peaceful space fills with soft laughter.
Small children, swaddled in black cloth, tied to mothers' backs.
Women eat hot tofu/*echakwe* from stalls as they spread their produce.

On green cloth: dried red peppers, ginger root,
tamarind leaves, garlic sprouts, chayote squash,
crabapples, fermented tea leaves, picked ginger,
sticky steamed blackrice, fried garlic, scallion, mashed—

              At night Shan drums beat.
                  Tattooed torsos writhe.
                      Kong, kong, kongo, kong.

Pagodas gleam pale in moonlight.
Saffron robed monks chant.
                                      Life is Dukkha!

Firefly nights—iridescent—as coupling fireflies   are swallowed by the   pale moon.

Piquant and Tart: Girlhood

night baths in open spaces.
drums filled with sunheated water.

sundays to shampoo long uncut hair.
her nipples dark purple.

        mine light brown with dark areolas.
        soft touches of tongue

smooth satiny sweet.

A hundred taste buds educate
on humid Taunggyi nights.

        lips explore, mouths entwined:
        piquant & tart.

Dusk in the mountains of Shan States

pagoda silver bells

ta ling ta ling ta ling

buffalos' wooden collars

ta laung ta laung ta laung

Shan kettle drums

kongo, kongo, kongo, kong.

Monks in Saffron Robes: Part One

monks   in   saffron   robes
march   for   human   rights

monks   in saffron   robes
protest   in   Rangoon

monks   in   saffron   robes
walk to   Shwedagon   Pagoda

monks in   saffron   robes
march to   Sule Phaya

monks in   saffron   robes
hold   placards   high

monks   in saffron   robes
float   in shallow   water

                                      Dead.

Destinies

body deprived of touch from loving hands
as palms spread out on back breast face

feeling withers wilts fades like mountain orchid
in hot Rajasthan desert where warm dust blows

& as the petals shred and scatter,
i collect and cradle them in my arms

for moments or lifetime or eons
for knowing and unknowing lovers.

2. exiles and dislocations: love, marriage and family

You and I: Interconnected beyond the Mountains

You sit on the sun warmed ground, your long white hair newly washed and spread around you like gossamer veils. Your brown-skinned face with its deep set eyes reassure me even after decades apart. When you disappear, when I close my eyes, when I reach out to touch you, how do you know to come back? The smell of Punjab rains, the mustard fields, your cow Janki, the newly churned butter, the carnival in the village—when was I there? Generations have gone by, but you continue to plow the fields and weave fabric and embroider colorful *phulkaris* for my half Korean granddaughter by the beach on the pacific ocean—ever knowing and *generative*.

Motherland

I remember leaving Taunggyi in early dawn,
stars still out, drinking sweet chai
spiced with cardamom,
suitcases and children loaded in truck,
our brown fragrant
limbs tangled.

      we looked at the silhouette
           of the mountains, at our home
                at the rushing, tumbling, burbling waterfall,
                      thinking of hand-mixed tofu salad wrapped

                                      in teak leaf.

            left our round-faced neighbors,
            their coconut chicken noodles,
            taste of sour mangoes with shrimp paste
            and mosquito-netted dreams
            in warm homemade quilts—

looking to our future
in India, our *Mulk*.

remember, father, born and bred in Burma, said,
*when you reach Calcutta, take the dust
of the land and smear in on your forehead,
your Motherland. Your home is no more.*

    After hours on the plane   across the sea,
    we made Calcutta—Dum Dum Airport.

older sister had fever, loss of home, refused to touch   earth   dust
to forehead.   I did, our motherland of strangely constructed
and alienated words:

I (In-between) N (Nothingness)   D (Dukkha) I (Illusions)   A (Aloneness)

Home is the diasporic who dances nightly in fragmentary shadowy spaces.

Delhi Girl

Mother, I go to college now,

        a Delhi girl.

    You do not like the way

           I dress.

    I have many more-than-friends.

        You tell Father,

           be careful.

Father laughs.

        All the while you sew us Delhi-style clothes:

           bellbottoms, *churidar kurtas*, tight *kameezes*.

Roots of Love and Barks of Desire

Love is a story told by grandmother BeyBey
of Hir and Ranjha, star-crossed lovers,

of a king losing his loving wife
in a game of dice, love is a tale

learned in the Convent School,
Romeo and Juliet, young and lost,

yet all desire to be enfolded
and become one with the beloved

& yearn to see from the windows
of the Other's soul, to be reflected

in the mirrors of colonial masters
and become "real," for light of knowledge

flies through even dense cloud
blankets of homegrown cotton fiber

dyed with roots of curcuma longa
and barks of madhuca indica,

stories sewn by countless female hands
whispered in the glow of earthenware lamps

in fabric woven in Punjab and Taunggyi
embraided with silken threads

    & dancing to the cold stone gods
            in shiva temples in ancient India,
                  the lover threads marigolds
                        for the stone necks, as if
                              the soft petals will rejuvenate
                                      a virgin married to a groom
                            by parents who then guide

　　　　　　　her to be like an Apsara in public spaces
　　　　while Kama Sutra is whispered,
　　nails on thighs, cardamon on breath,
in a congested room and smokefilled kitchen,

    as if the   bee   sucking   nectar
    can   turn it to   fragrant   honey
    simply by   nature,   when   the arts
    are   no   longer taught   but   are lost
in the urban   spaces of the   westernized world   beneath
crumbly
    bridges   smoggy megapolises   walled   sunless
    tenements   and   glass
    cages—

yet: love longs to touch,
heal, smell, kiss, fuck
    finds ways in narrow lanes
    of Indian and Burmese villages
    and towns to concrete beehives
    in modern cities like the sun:
    filling cracks in walls
    of old mud houses
    where village women draw
    white and blue tantric circles squares

on cow dung smeared mudded surfaces of their homemade
    homes for love to dwell in old copper pots
stirred with bay leaves, cinnamon
    and cloves, sautéing it with
scarred fingers
    caressing it with first milk of the cow
after birth, browning it with jaggery,
    refreshing, as is bathing at the seven springs:

naked young bodies splashing in cold
water as force of stream hits crowns
        of heads, naked mothers and grandmothers

                    in predawn shadows, rejoice in primordial
bathing rituals, dried crushed *kinpun* seeds
& soaked *tayaw* bark, facial scrub and shampoo
                            on tender and old flesh, long uncut hair
                    wet swaying beneath teakwood trees, before
the dawn and sunlight on Taunggyi mountains
as they return to the inner sanctum:

to marinate dreams of intimacy in juicy
tamarind and turmeric, slow cooked
in mud pots on padauk wood fires
in tiny kitchens, sitting on low stools
rolling *rotis* puffing them on embers
                    a dot of homemade ghee, as if love
                            melting on browned surface of skin
                            of the beloved, tenderly touched by the heat
                                    emanating from breath caught in layers
                                    of smoothly kneaded dough bought
                                            from farmer crushing wheat in waterwheel
                                            still warm to touch, fingers swirling
                                    as if: Apsaras dancing for Buddha
                                    to disrupt his meditation
                        : a female cobra, violently twisting
                    her body around the male in coitus
            as a coiled rope
        all the way to heaven
: a cat calling all night to her lover,
voice cracked and urgent with longing
        to be united with the prowling one
        : fish fillets roasted in fenugreek
                anise, coriander, mustard, cumin,
                nestling in saffron infused basmati rice
                        : secret meetings in borrowed homes,
                        fear and feast commingling in stranger's bed
                        as if destinies are not written but created on mauve
                        cotton sheets patterned by curving limbs,
                        for love is not only in bodies that meet
                but also in smoke that blows to lover's lips
                from centuries ago, from dreams of lives

       in mud huts and marbled homes, in next lives
       and re-memories, in re-imaginations
on top of snowcapped mountains
in the Shivaliks, in the crunch of snow
    and ice on Tian Shan mountain range,
       in slow cooked milk and rice
          flavored with pistachios, in chili spiced
              fermented tea leaves and crushed fried garlic,
              in feelings of baby's fingers around aged hands.

Love is in the smell,   breaths   and   heartbeats
of   day and night   of hopeful   eternities

and   lifetimes like   tender buds   of tropical yellow   tiger orchids

placed in coconut shells   lined with husks   tied to trunks of
dancing   avocado   trees.

Lost in Taunggyi

        You went purchasing cotton and rayon fabric to Rangoon,
told us tales from that place—
                the pagodas: Shwedagon, Sulay,
& the city people. Shami—the bakery, the open night markets'
    fried tofu and noodles.

Before the summer of 1962 was over, the Burmese military
    army trucks rolled up in front of our shop,
PJ Singh and Brothers, stole everything:
      the showcases, the safe, and especially the family's dignity.
            For years we took useless banknotes
in baskets and left them at the bank.

Father sold Ma's wedding jewelry to feed eighteen hungry mouths,
    a joint family, then took to illegal smuggling.

Chacha Saran imprisoned
    for six months in Mandalay/Insein prison.

            Ten-year old Daljit watched in horror
            from fragmented spaces, hid contraband

 in your shack in the Taunggyi market—our borders
    softened by dust, an aging mother's portrait,

eyes looking backward to estranged landscape
of dusty farmlands reimagined as emerald green,

and the years that separated us
    through the honeyed blackness.

Wings of *Hintha*

        an iron enclosure
                breath caught in throat
                      tied hands over my tender mouth
                              ears clogged with cotton wool
                      feet skimming green grass
              in *Hopong Yethwet*
            during *Tazaugmone*
    diwali   gurupurabh
in wide homemade flower patterned frocks   Shan sisters
    playing   tricks
        stories of reincarnation
              mountainloving father
                  carrying glee on shoulders
                        sharing life was his game.

I hid in   dark   shadowy   spaces,
    learning timidness from   gentle mountaincarrying   mother
who effaced her   efforts and   work
        so as not to appear   immodest
    strong in spirit but   weak in body
        she took humiliation   &
                survived

yet,   I misread her   modesty and   humility as   weakness

        I hid in   borders
            becoming
                  ashamed of my life force—
      my anger:
             links   binding   my hands
        broken
knock on   dark walls
      bit by tiny bit
            light seeps in—
my   hands   are   beautiful

An offshoot of the tree

from Gaya
(under which the Buddha
sat, meditated, and found
enlightenment)

rises above the golden spires
of Shewdagon Pagoda
in Rangoon
where a Burmese monk

in ochre robes   sits—

Swirling

turtle   hides   you
go down
the ocean's—blue:
white waves
heavy body's light
coming to my home—
presents a journey's warmth

        reflections are a reality:

    of touch and thought
    gliding from shell

& calmly through
scent of home and family,
& occasionally to she:

teaching now—sitting   by the   sea

New Arrivals: New Delhi

Days/nights blur
into busy bazaars and disparate
sensibilities: a mother's troubled gaze
searches lost daughters—

universities and crowded buses
overflowing rooms and untidy beds
gruel of *toor* dal and broken boiled rice
with fried dried chilis and green onions
sleepless nights or dreamless slumbers
on flat rooftops with wetsheets
to ward off the desert's hot *loo* winds
hunger assuaged by bits of watermelon
fed by aging and fragile grandmother
to tearfilled and disoriented granddaughters
estranged from land of birth and parents:

Shan buds never to bloom.
Chiaroscuro of smoldering glow
       between such dark spaces.

What is love, Ma?

*at your age, daughter, i had two children and a third
on the way, i had no time to dream.*

      yet i know you used to dream.

when i was a little girl, you told me love stories
of Amrita Pritam and Imroz:

      artist and poet—they transcended customs
      and creed, choosing a clean canvas to redraw fate.

      mornings, your hand in mine, we'd walk
      in the misty rain in Taunggyi.

You Talk Too Much

1.
Father, you took uncle's truck to the border,
                bought some fabric from Thailand,
started your trade again after the Partition,
        after displacement and exile
from India to Burma to India and back,
        had a small shop with rooms for us in the rear
 on the main road of Taunggyi.

2.
                      Was I born in that house?
            After two daughters and one son?
                You were disappointed.
                    A girl was born after me
and her beauty won your heart, Father.
        But you loved me, Mother:
        I was chubby and round cheeked.

3.
I started growing, tall and gangly,
                thick bushy eyebrows, skinny as a flat bedbug.
                      Who will marry her?
Mother, you would rope me in to crush garlic and ginger,
        and I'd cry and complain,
                      Why me?
You called me popcorn, going *pop, pop,*
        a goat producing milk but shitting in the bucket.

4.
Ma, did you eat a crow when you were pregnant with me?
                No, but you ate crow shit when you were little and that's why—
                                    you talk so much.
When I was a Delhi University student,   *I went on anti-dowry marches.*

               I wore torn jeans and tie-dyed shirts with red and blue glass beads

        and I draped the colorful scarf you knitted for me with yellow and purple
threads you brought back from Burma.

Border Wounds

a mother's world
            wounded by
                        border crossing
                                        trying to hold America:

                          refracting universe

              earth kissing land lost

      i envelop—

    transforming the home—you,

my daughter.

Bina
(named after a star)

Your baby curls, eyes brown, I remember
your small chubby hands and cherryred

> cheeks. My babysister, you were so very tiny.
> A fighter you became. We lost our country

and then our home; still we persevered.
We went from one nation to another

> and called them home. We were unhomed.
> Your gentle and loving face now strained

your healthy body ailing. *Cancer.* What
a terrifying word. Your lungs squeezed tight.

> Poison released perhaps from fracking in your home
> in Pittsburgh. Radon. Odorless. In soil and rocks.

Your cells. *Metastasis*. It spreads. poisonous
chemo floods your body—to heal.

> With each new dose it slams you down and out.
> Still rising fighting. You say, *don't cry. I will*
>
> > *be fine.* You're worried for family,
> > your children—I ask: *how are you?*

Liar: Two Raindrops

When you lie between two raindrops,
    May I lie with you?

Will we discover arid areas
    that we will roam

for sustenance—
    Or will we float on the crest

        of waves that drops create?

When you lie between two raindrops,
    may I lie with you: and discover infinity?

Will we discover stars between rain cloud breaks?
    Will we discover tropics with fruits—

        durians papayas mangosteens?

When you lie between two raindrops,
    will the swans swim with you amidst the floating lilies?

When you lie between two raindrops,
    I will lie with you:

        and re-discover truths of mating moonbugs.

Krishna: The God of Love

After five daughters,   one dead,
she goes to the Son-Born Hospital

in Taunggyi, neglected all night,
as no one accompanies her

for the birth, her husband says,
                                           of another badluck daughter.

She finally gives birth before morning.

She touches: the baby's face, arms,
legs, rubs them to warm the cool skin.

Her fingers, enfeebled with the
prolonged labor, massage the body

in the cold predawn hours.
As exhaustion and sleep overcome her,

she envisions her baby suckling:
her breast, touching her dark skin

with tiny fingers, skin only brutalized
                                           by rape & by slaps and fists.

She awakens with a start and sees
that her eleven pound blue skinned baby boy,
                                           Krishna, lies dead by her side.

Home

(cutting ties means abandoning family and
culture, finding means and meanings in alternate
stories and narratives reconstructing
self and community. Other ties, other
tales, other families. or isolation and defeat.
small resistances and small goals.
deep breath and fresh eyes. a new
day. reading and seeing anew.)
alone but not lonely anymore
collective loss individual gain.

Famine & Plentitude

plentitude in strawberry fields
bamboo village cherry-covered hills

childhood frolics in blue-belled Taunggyi meadows
afternoon teas fried tofu & sweetened condensed milk

soaked with homemade bread and *puris*
long morning walks on pine trees Grey Stone

swims in cool and deep Hopong springs
long tangled hair sunning on warmed rocks

lungi covering tender budding breasts
young. Browned torsos slumbering

on homemade quilts, mother & grandmother's laps
father's tender gazes touching shy eyes

broad shoulders carrying mountains of glee
idyllic turned alien alienated in motherland:

tanged jungles of dust & hunger in Delhi
streetside Romeos bruising fragile buds of Shan

dirty old men feeding famished sitting ducks
mansions adorned with naked aging wife's portrait

Maharaja of this and that—
disco nights drugs excitement of guilt

at abandonment of home
slumbering in stranger's beds

to belong, mother father haven to re-turn
voided darkness Delhi nights narrow streets

of immigrants, Shan buds never to bloom
crumbled scattered on deserts of India

to reemerge blossoming in arid land
submerged & repressed now readjusted

never forgotten glimpse of paradise
apsaras in mundane mask camouflage

appearing in dark spaces
skulking stalking shadows

playful marauders, knower of glances
touch tied trying to show

glimpses of paradise lost
in fallen angel's piercing glance

tortured
                tantalizing
                        tearful laughter
                                sorrowful
                                        light ricocheting
                                on rain swept Ashok Vihar lanes
on moonless monsoon nights.

Ganga Ghats

from a rowboat pulled by young
baba kumar sahni, as the sun
transforms to a five-armed goddess,
I watch five and seven pandits
perform *arti* on Ganga Ghats.
Hundreds of bells swing
in incensed air releasing Aryan songs.

diyas swaying dozen arms hold flames aloft,
as sun sinks in sacred polluted river.
green pipal leaf cupping candles flames float,
as small boys in canoes carefully place them
in waves. hands clap when sandlewood smoke swirls
in frenzied plumes, marigold petals
scattering for Ma Ganga as she is tucked
in by the devotees for the night.

        I spark candles one by one
        and slip them in leaf cups, offer
        them for the world, the water.
        they slip and rock in the currents.

bodies stripped
to ash and dipped in holy water—

I smell flesh burn.
watch dead bodies contort.

remains placed in water rock and sway:
                someday   to return.

Border Wars and Enlightened Love

A young mother, pregnant with our second child,
I flew to war-torn Iraq with our four-year old daughter,

Gitanjali (named after a poem), to be with the father
who was working in Bagdad to earn a living—

she was born through a C-section in the Doon Valley—
her father absent, at work, in Orissa—and I,

alone and in labor for days, wanted the second child
to be born in his presence even as Iraq was in turmoil:

territorial wars over Stream of the Arab
at the confluence of River Tigris and Euphrates

Soviet and US supplied armaments devasting both
while remaining *neutral* in the long brutal war

to keep oil rich areas in the Persian Gulf
from being dominated by the Arabs or Persians—

& unable to sleep nights with skin allergies and fear,
I sat by the open windows & watched tankers roll by

on pain darkened streets of Baghdad al-Jadida
dusk skies torn by loud jet sorties through highways in the sky:

> our son was born at the Red Crescent Hospital—Hilal Al Ahmer—
> filled with wounded bodies of the soldiers

as blood spilled in Iraq and Iran, homes draped in black sheets
where young Shaheeds were daily *celebrated*

with music and food by bereaved families—
I cradled him in my arms, son of an exile from Burma,

grandson of the Partition refugees, & at a ceremony
in a Sikh shrine in the Karkh District of Bagdad,

where, in 1520, on his way back from Mecca-Medina,
Baba Nanak sang of one light in all beings:

we named him Gautam after Buddha
and Mohan after Krishna: *Enlightened Love.*

3. diasporic peregrinations: myriads encounters

Gray Ocean Pearl: From Tennessee to California

Ravi Shankar's slow sitar music
filled warm Jackson Tennessee night,

as I talked about an artist
visualizing dark skin long hair

patient as the moonbeams
a laidback lizard on sunbathed land,

unflappable as snowcapped Himalayas.
I now sit contemplating nearly dark years

cracked shells and crooked bones
familiarities of years and lifetimes

crust half filled with Pacific Ocean waters
in sunfilled rainstarved golden beaches

sand grain turning deliberately
existence vibration pulsating emerging

oyster's painful treasure to gray pearl
caressed by salty polluted sea waters.

Vasco da Gama: Oil Lamps and Stars

Vasco da Gama and the teeth of stars
        flashing in their mischief,
                the earth a living feast—

        like Columbus and his pointing
     fingers—

being in Goa,
and seeing the reflection of Portugal in it—
      transformed.

                Goans use oil lamps,
anoint their foreheads, knees, skin,
      at the St. Francis of Assisi's church—

Long lines of devotees to glimpse the saintly lover of animals
      lying in a silver box—

                Thousands stand there
to see the one they believe brought Jesus to their shores.

Kynsna

I.
Twilight in Kynsna Estuary
Umtata Windhoek Server
on paddle cruiser—
I glide
past svaroski crystal-studded
Thesen and Leisure Isle
to western head featherbed
tolling emerald peridot.

II.
Foucault and Mda companions
from individual to communal
finding meaning in Protea's petals:
separate development, Bantu education—
Mahatma's generations in Durban
and Cape Town replicating Salt March:
Immorality and Mixed Marriages Acts—
sharing women motherhood in the diaspora.

III.
Teachers of disenfranchised Cape Coloureds
strolling along in Kirstenbosch gardens
King Shaka Zulu's children
transformed in Madiba's Land.

IV.
Poverty-stricken in first world bubble
Gugulethu, Laanga, Soweto, Pheonix
tin shacks in cold blowing Kaap Staad winds.
scholars at University of Cape Town
emulate Buddha's interconnectedness
in Coetzee's *Disgrace*.

V.
I bleed my hemorrhaging skull like Antjie Krog.
Who will bring succor to the wretched of the earth?
Ah, Malika Ndlovu, bring us you me women
together growing in the shade.

Uluru-Kaja Tjuta National Park, Central Australia: Mother and Child

- *Tjukurpa stories, dots and dashes, linear, non-linear lines*
- *Uluru around which elders sit in C formation*
- *Marks made on ancient rock by ancestors as maps to live*
- *Dance, art, and sacred stories shared only with Anangu*

i find you:
mother and child—
sitting by the shopping center
outside the IGA grocery store
in the Uluru-Kaja Tjuta national park
your art spread out by the mosaic floor
as you crouch, not looking up,
nor making eye contact

                                                      the rich white tourist

        shows *cultural sensitivity* and sits on floor
        by your side, with iphone in hand
        talking to her daughter in Sydney
        showing photos of the art.

                Which one will go with the decoration in your house?

                I approach and the tourist explains to me:

                the artist is so kind, she allowed me
                to take photos of her art, so i could show
                my daughter for her selection.

mother with child explains the sacred meaning
of community and interconnections with plants, earth

                          after selection, she takes a photo with you.

        i buy the art with animals and dots
        and you ask for my pen to sign it,

        ask if i wish a photo,
        i ask the white tourist to take one,
        who keep insisting your two-year-old baby
        should be also in it. The mother, child and me.

you leave with your child.

minutes later, i feel the desire
to buy the smaller of your art pieces

                the white tourist tells me to follow
                you into the IGA, for certainly
                you are there, with money from the art
                purchasing some food.
for you and your child

red dots and black
circular lines and straight
C formation for sitting community
Ululu and Kaja Kjuta showing
way with formations and design

                Later, I meet the white tourist at a café
                and she, looking at another small Anangu child,
                says, *they are so beautiful, so exotic.*

                you know, she says, twenty years ago
                they would not have been allowed near the café
                they have only been given the privilege
                a few years ago by our government.

the space, sacred, now commercialized
tourists' footprints on sacred designs
i am complicit. i consume. Skin color
brown like Anangu exploits in   . . . colonized spaces . . .

Between Zambia and Zimbabwe

      the moving earth

           suddenly decided

                to stop

                      here

                            at the edge

                                    between a desert

                                            and a ravine

Cynthia, A Maid in South Africa

today, I ask Cynthia her South African name
Zanyiwe Nofests Mtshwana.

She is a Xhosa woman and works
for him going on twelve years

her room where she sleeps weekday nights
is filled with his storage stuff.

in the corner, she has two boxes
with all her material possessions.

last week, her house in the township
was looted and burned, so now

the boxes are all that she is left with:
two dresses, a coat and one sweater.

two blouses, one red and one white.
two skirts, one black and one blue.

one book. The bible.

Kars: Pale Moon in Thunder

Shepherds living in huts covered with mud   where green grass grows on roofs for warmth.

Northeastern Anadolu Anatolia, I see Georgian Armenia where   statue respecting unity is torn

down by the government   where cheese and honey flow while Shepherds freeze in shacks

both communities share common food: *kofta kababs, dolma, mezes, kunefe*

yet Turks, Kurds, Armenians are separated by fear—

A hailstorm pelts the city and drums on ancient roofs
                                      in city of Kars where lighting and thunder strike.

A pale moon rises over the Armenian Hills on Turkey's horizon   w h e r e in ancient Armenian city of Ani, ruined eleventh century mosques, churches, palaces are reflected:

in the still and silent Kars River.

Halong Bay

Floating on a vintage "Indo-China" junk boat
cruising Vietnam's famous bay
lunching on delicious fish and mangoes
a white tourist from New Zealand
says, *what can you expect in Vietnam?*
as he buys a bottle of water for two US dollars.

Biting into the ripe mango,
I say, sarcastically—
Welcome to the Third World!

Arching his white eyebrows, he replies,
Well, they know how to
fleece the First World!

Relishing the golden flesh of the fruit
I add, *it was the First World that*
fleeced the Third World first.

The warm breeze brushes my face
as I sit gazing at emerald waters
limestoned Stone Dog and Teapot islets
rainforests on the tops of mountains
towering above us.

They call them *Paisa, Chavanni, Athani*

There were three abandoned girls, ages five,
six and ten. They came to the rural Sikh ashram

of Older Sister, who, bent by birth, raised by faith
a sage healer, (not) a true Sikh, she now

keeps a relic of long passed *Sant's*
worn shoes and clothes in special prayer room.

And scores of ailing old and young people
form a line outside her red door. She sits

on a red carpet, muslin scarf on hair.
Her feet are bare. They touch them, heads bowed

> and place wads of money at her fragile feet.
> Using the dead Sikh sage's Gold and Red shoes,
>
> she rubs them on their heads and backs. Supine,
> or bent, they live at her feet for days.

She runs a school for girls and women,
who, young and formerly abused,
are now healed by Older Sister.

The new girls' names are: *Penny, Quarter and Dollar.*

Ocean of no return

- i dream life in bits and pieces
mountain climbs, spiced goat curry,
afternoon slumbers in rainy seasons,
swinging from tropical vines,
leaving home, feeling estranged

- i imagine that time is here and now
for loving days, finding lifelong friends
sharing laughter, tears like black salt,
smiles like molasses and cherries

- i love desire and fun. i crave bliss
to merge and emerge, one with one,
mirth and play, shadowy selves
nirvana and awareness of enlightenment

- i see lively pleasures offer momentary release,
disco and dancing, reflected and refracted
colorful lights, borrowed homes and beds,
borrowed lovers and life-mates in estranged
rhizomic stories and glass rooms

- i feel sexy touches pass us by daily flee
like rainbow nights, embroidered shadows
& torn roots, floating lilies, muddied waters
and growing in flashes of green light

- i think only we are dreaming life, it floats,
in samsara and maya, illusions of life
of webbed realities, silken shades of
gossamer wings & flying green ants

- i contemplate time floats, swims,
it crawl sideways, like crabs
slithering in crevices and waves
in ether of caves and boulders

- i find life is here, then gone astray,
swirling, whirling, and dancing
without strings, the marionette
balances on cliff top tree roots
drifting into the ocean of no-return

Learning to sing like never before

silence at skin touches
stillness at caught breath

as if Carolina evenings
dance in sacred rural farms

unfocussed eyes seeing sense,
as trepidation heightens impression

breaking received thoughts
& riding wind like a longtailed kite

drifting on warm breeze
songs muffled to muted tunes

a hum, a refrain, a slow gathering
of stringed musical movements

unknown sensations tapping throat
sliding down curve of neck

& back of knees, as a sudden spring night
denotes sweetness and cool rain

when a pine tree pins a half moon
in the bluish half night sky.

In Search of Nothingness

To be
empty—
nothingness
is absolute reality:
devoid of any lasting substance
we are interconnected.

A void is not pure negation,
it is serene vibrancy—*sunyata*.

Life is an illusion, *maya*
Love is *maya* Suffering is *maya* Pain is *maya*.

Therefore, to desire
is to suffer—*Dukkha*.
True *sunyata*
is not
a state of voidness.

Compassion is—*Karuna*.

We are nothing in ourselves,
  interconnected,
    where no fears exist is—*Nirvana*.

Fuchsia Tea

Today, collecting blossoms of fuchsia
                from scarred skin of my sacred lover,
                      I brew a cup of fragrant tea.

      tracks are not to be followed
                          but made
      tracks are not to be contemplated
                          but embraced
tracks are not a road map
                          but traces
of life's stings and songs.

I pour a cup of tea.

Oregon's Crater Lake

Mount Mazama
erupted creating crater
holding water trust wraps around
mauve-colored flowers on pumice as sap
flows through petals lake's breeze
emanating joy suspended
eternity in Lava
rocks.

Walking in Two Worlds

Michigan breeze blows long hair over mouth
taste of wood floating in Superior
through pine-encrusted Peninsula
smells of woodsmoke sweat sage.

An eagle gliding between emerald new-leafed trees
raven's wings glisten darkblue
remembering our passage once before.
Ancestors walk on sacred path

a cow on sun baked muddy estuary
continuing Punjabi legacy
walking in two worlds.
Unearthing knowledge of downtrodden

to subvert past through reconfigured saga
intermingling genealogies in disparate continents
watched over by departed souls to lick monsoon
rain on face of the beloved again someday.

Raat Ki Rani

wandering up & down the old victorian home
and looking for the tall hidden turret,

i plant seeds of fragrant blossoms,
Queen of the Night, blooming

pure white, emanating musky odor
and attracting colorful moon bugs,

they are unable to distinguish,
you, me, us, they, too, are confused.

A Coiled Serpent Speaks

A long and coiled serpent speaking tonight,
the mouth of night is mute. The stars are staring

in wonder blank. The sky is spreading cold
and clear shawl over the sleeping mute earth.

I listen to the deadly truths that are
muted slumbering whispers, the beaten

music of thumps on backs that are so sore
burdened by weight of centuries. Shielding

the truth from harsh westerly winds
tearing at tender shoots for future gen-

erations, mysterious about twisted
and tangley webs of minds that gently sway

and bending, lying low in swamps fetid/
fertile. A coiled serpent speaks to the night.

The heart of night slowly splits into two:
to hundreds pomegranate red seeds bleed

secrets that are then told to strangers' night.

Eyes that do know the words that mouth barely
dare whisper. Keepers of the knowledge and

bearers of broken wounded psyches, that
are wandering earth in flowers roots and leaves.

I hold the bud in palm of hands, and crouch
in earth and dust where coiled serpent slowly speaks.

Ripples

Today, an eternity of threat wrapped
in hazel eyes, a lynx predator,
high on top of Maltnomah Falls
                      mist spraying dizzying peaks—

fantasies, of night lights and loud music
or eternal sunshine on Venice Beach,
                      like Malibu Creek Canyon, fade—

as the sun rises and fog lifts,
strokes of falcon's wings,
                      on Oregon Cascades—

Drops of water from fern-covered rocks
at Mary's Peak, reflect clouds
and mountains of Douglas fir, Oregon sea lions in caves
                      sunning on rocks—

an opening on an ancient shore,
a lost animal searches its mundane
world and a crack appears.

Then, drop by drop, as condensation falls on earth
where pomegranate blossoms red,
each kernel of crimson fruit
                      a piece for childhood playmates—

becoming familiar melodies,
like child knowing touch of mother alone,
                      ripples in oceans—

waves, unaware of water lying underneath,
washes over unknown feet
                      at Devil's Churn.

Counting Blessing

1. whispers of mountain pagoda bells on still moonlit nights
2. fireflies dancing in balmy twilight, landing on soft palms
3. twinkling lights creating swirls of feelings half un-remembered
4. a child's seeking finger holds a tender multicolored butterfly
5. colors sprinkle on little fingertips golden-brown black speckles
6. a rainbow over a waterfall spraying blessings onto faces
7. kindled flame threatening to engulf warm days, nights of skin
8. Taste of fish *mohinga, laphat tot*, and green papaya salad
9. mountains whispering cherry blossoms and grey stone falls
10. the self trying to open tiny buds to create a kaleidoscope of light
11. trees reaching the cloudless sky in the Shan Mountains.

Appeasing the Goddess

A bird devours
              hidden stories   &   you feel
                                                           its wings laden
      appeasing
                   the goddess
                             in invisible webs   as   s/he

                     brews a hot cup of   tea   served
with limpid eyes.

                         In sweet syrupy   watermelon—

                                                     a fly is stuck.

A Riddle for You

what is the foam on the crest of the waves: *a dance*
what is the mist on top of the mountains: *a ghost*
what is the leaf that falls from the tree: *a renewal*
what is the pressure from a newborn's fist: *a contemplation*
what is the glimmer in eyes of the beloved: *a story*
what is the thread that holds the fabric: *a generation*
what is the drop of water on a lotus leaf: *a faith*
what is the osprey that follows your raft: *a guide*
what is the rapid that brings the white water: *a reckoning*
what is the water that flows through a spring: *a tempo*
what is the sound that comes from a flute: *a beckoning*
what is the string that a musician strums: *a vibration*
what is the breeze that blows at the ocean: *a lifeline*
what is the song on the lovers' lips: *a chance*
what is the jingle on the bride's anklets: *a promise*
what are the scales on the floating silver fish: *a serenity*
what is the grass you lie on in the Cascades: *a succor*
what is the whistle blowing through windy pines: *a history*
what is the snow that melts on eyelashes: *a dream*
what is the paint on top of the brush: *a destination*
what is the prayer that is answered: *a continuation.*

Time signature

trumpeting jubilantly
Seal's breathe:
don't cry, tonight
my baby.

      crossing bridges
      lessons learnt
      amalgamating
      in third space

            identities
            eastern western
            no longer concrete
            material

                  to be momentarily
                  eternal & playful
                  childhood memories
                  a prayer for life force:

                        pulsating beats of Upland Coquis
                        in Puerto Rican rainy nights.

4. into the sunset: or, circling back

Immigrant

i welcome morning snow
on skeletal trees, softly
blowing turtledoves
descending & settling
on pure white ground.

remembering bamboo
village Taunggyi meadows,
afternoon teas, fried tofu,
swims in Hopong springs,
i welcome fragmented sky
scattering the snowy night
& the sensation of lost
pinecovered mountains
jacaranda blossoms,
piquant tart mangoes
& mangosteen. i recall
fragrance embedded
in brown skin of lovers.

moon's frozen tears piercing breast.

Moon's frozen tears piercing breast.

Moonlit Nights

Moon shimmering on   Superior surface   mistily intense

                                                           fingers writing poetic notes

     mired in earthly
                passion

                         chakor's enthrallment with the moon

illusion evaporate
                snoozing losers   slow blowers

       immerse ourselves in nothingness

                   drenched in suchness thusness—*thathatha*—nowness

     climes unknown
              melting snow on sunfilled fields

                                    moonsurfaced face
cascading waterfalls

     playful dark darkness
                     dancing on silveredged   Superior's
         depth

Seal's lyrics bridges   bridging Mackinac

                               bearing us all the way to Sault

     miasma forming kiss
             flute of Krishna's

        to submit   turbulently   quiescent in   moonlit masquerade
of tingling spaces

     safelanding from   moon's head's outerspace

       by inverting and inventing new paradigms

                           & toppling from perch on high.

A Dark Grain of Sand

darkness hides moon
grimly pirouetting shadows

dance on pained breast's surface
words emptied of meaning
fear-driven whirl
swirl

plummeting from high scalp
dreaming space
reneging on promise

outstretched hands withdrawn
at the last nanosecond of descent

flaying specter
splashing ice cold Superior's berg
on idealized
ocean's unconcerned surface

a grain of nondescript sand
splintered
for no one's sake
and   sank.

Emptiness

swirling specters
dissipate halfway
some remained
turning playful
mistily
appearing
from abyss
craggy darkness
reflecting glow
of unrepentant lover
now there now gone
psyche splintered
myriad constellations converge
birthing triangle of Bermuda
into eternity
of no-self
in micromoments
landscapes of desires
nightmares
corroding
death's breath
for eternity
wrapped in tiny
sand grain's essence
of multitudes

& emptying self of ego
like fragrance the flower
& flower the fragrance

nestled in palm
inverted.

Plentitude

        I touch
        plentitude not yet
        turned to bliss
        returns to source
        written words
        sound of voice
        now a touchstone
        rambunctious
        bud
        suspended
        in the in-betweenness
        of potentiality
        of laden clouds
        on bare skin
        blanket of desire
        wildriverbear's bare body
        surface reflecting moonlit
        Marquette nights.

Healer

You heal, scarlet orchid,
hanging on tropical tree,

moonlight on Superior waters
and slow circling gull,

iridescent white sand particle
under arch of wet foot,

softly trailing fingertips
on hot buttered cornbread,

sun ripened apricots, peaches
strawberries in warm climes,

angels dancing on luminescent clouds
sprinkling stardust on little people

sharing secret rituals of prehistoric ones,
tiptoeing prancing circling magical tree

allowing black crested Indian bubul
to nest on the branches of Lombardi.

Turtle, Turtle in the Sea

Turtle, turtle in the sea, are you playing
hide and seek with me? You go up and you
go down. Are you playing hide and seek with me?
the ocean's blue, the waves are white, your neck

is small and sticks over crest of waves,
your heavy body seems so light and strong,
going down and up and going around,
turtle, turtle in the sea, are you coming

home with me? Or, are you playing hide and seek
by being present the moment life is but a
journey through the sea, warm reflections warmer
reality? Then thoughts and ideas glide

from shell, remaining calm as you, fighting
roughly calm waters, glide towards me.
Turtle, turtle in the sea, where is home
and family? Appearing and then disappearing,

do you come and go as you please,
or do you go home occasionally to—she?
turtle, turtle in the sea, playing hide
and seek with me. teach me how and teach

me now. i ride the waves and swim the sea,
expose my tender neck and head. just to
have met you, i'm so glad, sitting by the sea.
turtle, turtle, will you come home with me?

Weathering It

tropical day's warmth
but so much more appealing

monsoon showers tickle
barely emergent flowers

                                  as rains

the autumn leaves
burn skin to brown

passion will not be declined:
after monsoon rain

the idea:
remains in lines—

stroked and etched
in hunger of   skin.

Dance like Rumi

when your steps become your destiny:
      stay—like you are in a warm country

when your thoughts become like dew:
      bathe—like you are washing dust of centuries

when your face becomes like the beloved:
      touch—like you are reunited after rebirths

when your words begin to arouse:
      caress—like the images are on fire

when the rain slakes the thirst of sand grains:
      drown—like levees on the river are breached

when the dung beetle pushes the lump of earth to its mate:
      fornicate—like the fight to death to reproduce

when the swan forgets to fly to its lover:
      crime—like the hunter's bow hits the target

when the mirror no longer reflects your face:
      walk—like a stranger in a foreign land

when the beloved no longer hears your voice:
      whisper—like hummingbird's wings in the wind

when the fish becomes fermented in the sun:
      explode—like flavors of sticky rice and chili peanuts

when the tealeaves float to the top of the hot water:
      blow—like the boat on the Irrawaddy river

when the cherry blossoms bloom on the flat mountains:
      sing—like the sailor who beckons you at each port

when the snow blows and settles on your eyelashes:
      taste—like dreams entering you through your mouth

when you take two turtle doves and set them free:
                    age—like you are a hundred-year-old mother of freedom.

Military Coup in Burma: Again

sanderlings, avocets, pelicans,
& gulls circle the crested waves
at Marina Del Rey beach
silhouetted by Santa Monica Mounts

when i pick up a half-hidden sand dollar
from the pacific coast and pocket it
& grains of sand dust my gnarled
fingers, lined palms, age spots

a remembrance of times gone by
but living within me each moment
and I think of another land, faraway
in the land of the greenghosts

where a military coup toppled
the democratic government, *again,*
& the golden sands of Ngapali
and the Bay of Bengal waves

crash against the tawny shores:
      & crabs scuttle sideways to death.

Rebirth
(After Ada Limón's "Before")

Fully dressed, but shabby,
wind in my hair, I walk
as an adult
behind the shadow
of my young mother.
After the marriage.
After the old house.
After the chopped stump.
After the divorce.
After the rubies in the safe.
After the bird's wings.
After the pantry filled with spices
by the vendor. After the flight
above us was the flight
from each of us, and I was
almost too small to remember
and lifted my arms:
Chandni Chowk, narrow lanes
between us, warm *loo* breeze,
strong muscles, and I
always knew abandonment
was different. Remembering past
lives with her, if I die,
to meet, once again, my mother
is what I yearn.

Moonlit Superior Shores to the Cascades:
A Journey Continues

Foam on top of the waves in moonlit Superior:
        bubbles of hope in tumultuous times
mist skimming the surface of water:
        tender blankets of down in freezing night
fall leaf floating on the crest of the waves:
        old life feeling buoyant on young shoulders
life on the shores of a mighty lake:
        moving with its flows and mist
becoming a wise old crone:
        breathing in and out with its rhythm

I arrived on Superior's shores
        with my dreams in my crumbly hands
half broken, half rescued
        a life lived as wife and mother
like bubbles on waves smashed
        by bigger waves on the sandy shores—

tonight, I collect fear and hope in boxes
        shipped to a new place yet unknown
like an aimless boat on the horizon
        picking up roots to find new soil
hoping for shoots to sustain another life
        in an old place by the Cascade Mountains.

The Haunting

        a million miles on rocky grounds . . .

            originally lean and wild

                  amidst tropical and humid forests

on blistered feet and   an empty woven bag to reach   the dream space . . .

       your Other Shadowed Self

           beckons you from the land splintered

                through conquest and wars   the excesses

                          turning it into a mere

           container of empty possibilities like

   —the clothbag and   *ghee rotis:* layered and rolled . . .

to be stared at as an oddity
                  —sometimes (away in distant
                                  border town for food)

              you turn into a freak:
dreaming of markets and
            the Goddess of Love

     in American opportunities

        where private parts

              are to be studied
                      and exhibited

     for everyone in this so-called dreamplace—

                  to see the truth in the Mirror.

Civilizing Mission
(After Norman Dubie's "The Kingdom")

a loud assertion
a command
to speak about poverty
and gender
in public spaces
celebrating the West.
a Lion in the desert
like Lawrence of Arabia
bringing women
to a paradise
by rescuing:
"the brown woman
from the brown man."

no one cares.

Chakwal, Punjab: Great-Grandmother's Ancestral Village

A tall thin figure,
her loose black *salwar kameez*
flapping against her legs.

Her *chunni* fluttering behind her
& a vulture circles above.

She turns at the corner of the field,
looks back at the twilight horizon:
solitary dark cloud drifting aimlessly.

> *No sight of her son. He promised*
> *to return from Burma. Take her with him.*

The mango fruits, hard and sour
on the tree, dangle and sway.

Suddenly, a crow caws from the tallest branch,
swinging to and fro, crying desolately, *"Kaa . . . Kaa."*

The Wisest One
(After Naomi Shibab Nye's "What Kind of Fool Am I?")

Remaining silent with a vengeance,
braiding her long gray hair
each night in bed,
first in Punjabi, turbulent clouds
of discordant notes as Partition
wrests her due to new borders,
then in Burmese, in borrowed,
but fluent language: *Just as it is!*
They'd whisper, removing themselves
from his pungent aura for the dark night.
And she took away our rights, so that
we become wise, needed or not, and
soon, which we haven't for a long time,
always, a mother's greatest insight—

This curse.

Dislocated: Down the Rabbit Hole

       originally lean and wild
                                                   becoming flightless

//over three and half centuries
       in impenetrable rainforests

     & in the Indian Ocean, transforming itself
       on the volcanic Island of Mauritius

     amidst tropical and humid forests
       //morphing into a museum piece,

           conquest's excesses
                 turning it to a mere

  dodo—and like this creature
       to be stared at as an oddity

to be studied or exhibited—
       like: Saartje Bartmann

           or: Sara Baartman
                 a Khoikhoi woman

           turned into a freak:
                 "Hottentot Venus," not

the Roman Goddess of Love
       but the one from the Gamtoos valley

           tourists touching her body and private parts
               for a fee, & like the Dodo, exhibited and

                                      beckoning flightless
exposing *myself* in belly of the beast.

On Gratification
(After Traci Brimhall's "Dear Thanatos")

Today, a goddess of carnal pleasure and lust
shimmered as a reflection on the lake
as she lived her pleasure

Taking the reflected image in her hands,
which should have dissolved to liquid,
she danced with her funky doppelganger

I condone this. The symbolic order disrupted.
I am the speaking subject.

Once, a lost meaning returned to haunt the speaker,
no longer fragmented but whole, it cohered—

a lover for all seasons, she lures with promises of ecstasy,
whose heart now recites the Kama Sutra
with promises of nirvana

Hers is an expansive desire. It embraces creativity.

On the beaches of Marquette, my mirror image came to me—
Luscious: full of poetry and stories.

Drawing Circles and Lines

As if: in swirling blue lights meaning is etched
in tender shoots and gnarled fingers
in brown soil, scratching significance
as if: words flow through fissures in earth
looking towards hazy, distant silhouettes
as if: a gauzy curtain is slowly parting
treetops rustle and flower petals shiver
as if: opening space between ribs
for fragrance and thorns rupturing cells
counting moments for pressure on worn hands
as if: eternity is a look in innocent eyes.

No longer fragmented

i   hold   sun   in   the   palms of   my aged hands

                         shimmering   on the Arabian   sea

       caught in   Chinese   fishing   nets:

i meet my shadow—

as   she   untangles   her body   from silken webs

       in the   setting sun: she becomes   me—

                       i am her.

Home for *Echakway*

Early morning sun shines on muddy Rangoon River,
                         as motorized barges roar by rocking fishing boats.

I take a side car, a rickshaw, pulled by a Burmese man
                         who cycles me through traffic to a small street teashop.

Daw Mi, selling hot echakway, my breakfast from home,
                         twists fermented dough, drops it in hot sizzling oil.

Wraps it in a piece of Burmese newspaper served with hot red tea
                         sweetened with condensed milk. I savor nostalgia.

Homes and Hearts: I have left behind

I miss you:
like anthills   the Savannah
doum palm   the dry Sahara
blue rain   the monsoon clouds

I think of you:
like first dreams of snowflakes entering eyelashes
as salve, first orange light touching Superior
as a sturgeon leaps, a bride adorning
hands with henna as dolak drum beats,
silver anklets jingling in lovers' new home
on an old wooden bed adorned
with blockprinted peacock blue spread.

I love you:
like yellow fall leaves on Brockway Mountains,
as if slowly drying turmeric roots, handmade jewelry
with Superior' gold agate rocks, as if sunshine
pools on wet lotus leaves, the Abbots' Jampot
thimbleberry jam at Eagle Harbor, as if black pearls
on warm brown skin, flat rocks in Canyon Falls
where iridescent dragonflies dance while mating,
as if playful green and yellow northern lights.

I feel you:
like baby's small fist in careworn hands,
as if larvae in cocoon, first fragile green shoots
under frozen Marquette grounds, as if tongue touches
nectar after a long famine, the gentle lapping waves
at McCarty's Cove, as if a baby suckling breasts,
view of Seven Sisters and thousands of stars,
as if protecting sailors on misty nights
navigating treacherous waves.

I touch you:
like cool wrinkled hands on feverish foreheads,
as if first snowfall on a Douglas fir, kneaded dough
rolled into chappatis and puffed on iron

skillet, as if clouds on a monsoon day, homemade butter
churned in earthenware clay pots,
as if dancing dervishes in Turkey.

I taste you:
like goatmilk chai with crushed anise, cloves,
cinnamon and ginger, rasmali in reduced thickened
milk with shaved almonds, as if tongue wrapped around
beloved's toes fingers earlobes nipples.

I fear you:
like a weeping virgin in Carolina pine forest decorating tree
with gold earrings bracelets at leaving her beloved's visions,
a red truck stuck in rural mud dug out by a southern farmer
for the hybrid illicit lovers, flags of myriad colors
in all white neighborhoods in wooded lanes by lake,
lone brown body isolated in glass cage and sealed windows,
an irate husband on track of lost wife who made herself disappear
at Pictured Rocks on a sunny summer Michigan day.

I dream of you:
like lost Shangri-La to find blind ecstasy in your earthly huts,
as if young hands decorating mud walls anticipate rebirth,
a sadhu meditating for years on one foot at the foothills of the Shivalik,
as if Shiva, Parvati and Ganesha will reappear,
cascading tannin Tahquamenon waterfalls surrounded by golden leaves,
as if a misty flower awaiting the bumblebee of love in late autumn.

I forget you:
like an old sage who waits, eternally scanning the horizon for beloved
who never left, a mendicant her path, as if all lanes leads nowhere
and everywhere, a crone her perceptions, as if all learned sagacity
was within her from the beginning,

    a yogini   a void   nothingness.

here, amidst echoes of baby laughter, where ocean waves
crash on seashells, where a pelican glides on soft wings,

a mortal in an alternative alley under a tropical gum
is still, as if a bioluminescent moonbug
in Waitomo cave spins & drops web
to patiently fish for gnats in
still . . . glowing . . .waters.

Climbing Malibu Creek Canyon

a seeker, touching, looking for crevices,
footholds handholds slow energy concentrated

> to go up slow inch by exhilarating inch
> trust has to be complete to reach the top

i remember the rock's energy, years ago,
my slippery fingers, dusting chalk from hippouch

> trying to grip and momentary losing concentration
> seeing a deep treacherous chasm muscles aching

my breath deep to recover feelings in lungs,
trying again tentatively griping small indentation

> i felt again my loosening fingers as trust was lost
> & reluctantly giving up, i slid down the rope

bowed down my head to the gray stone's power
recognizing its complicated topography

> yet rejoicing in its vast oceanic depth and breath
> & keeping image of boulder in my consciousness:

every known fissure crevice foothold handhold—
maybe next time i would discover a new way

> i recall laying myself down on the dry grass,
> warming myself in the Californian sunshine

& flexing new formed aching sinewy muscles
i believed in the ability to reach height:

> > one day.

Monks in Saffron Robes: Part Two

monks in   saffron robes
march against Burmese   Muslims

monks in   saffron robes
march   to *protect*   Burmese   *race and religion*

monks in   saffron robes
hunt   in   Rangoon

monks in   saffron robes
forbid   Burmese women   from marrying Muslims

monks in   saffron   robes
attack   the practice of   *halal*

monks in   saffron robes
deny   anti-Muslim   violence

monks in saffron   robes
      saw hundreds of   Rohingyas—

                                                        Dead.

Home is the Diasporic

I.

                                                  Half a backward look,
                                          half a touch to reach you

                           half a sigh as tree sheds bark
                           half a breath at tender greens

                 half a laden breast,
                 half a quickened step

unfolding petals shed,
enfolding fragrance within

a little balm here,
a flame of the forest there

stranger friends,
friends estranged

tastebuds hunger,
while flavor explodes

here my skin frissons, and there
it exfoliates to expose the real.

Where to now, oh traveler?
Home is forever lost,

yet you are now home.

II.
Last day in Delhi   of long time ago   to which I   "returned,"
     a refugee from Burma   I made you   my home   of paradoxes
of   hungry   college years
of   bemused   wedding ceremony   and late night   dancing
of   returning to parents,   a young mother
Delhi,   I left you,   migrating to the Land of Dreams

children   estranged from   land   of   birth
     celebrating   stolen   moments
        was disturbing   and magically   profound.
you   became a mother   on whose bosom

        I slumbered and   dreamed:
a demon   with colorful talons
        you   resonated

                                                within.

III.

Not yet whole,
but no longer
fragmented—
I wait
to become real
on cold Superior
shores—
where sunlight
dances over cold waves
moonbeams shimmer
over old oredocks
finding familiar objects
in boxes
locating myself:
       in long lost mementoes
       in Shivalik and Kanchenjunga
       mountains:
       floating on Inle Lake
       taste of jalebis in Chandni Chowk

gulls circling
Picnic Rocks
leaping waves
on boulders
demanding human
sacrifices—

        I bow down to it.

Acknowledgements

I would like to thank Patricia Killelea, one of the most critical, creative, scholarly and spiritual persons I had the good fortune to meet, to work with, and to get to know and who, during the enriching knowledge-and-craft-seeking journey, transformed me into a poet while becoming my soul sister. Thanks to the mercurial and magical Matthew Gavin Frank who made every piece of writing a fascinating journey into the unknown, but exciting, parts of the writing process and who has become the dearest sojourner to explore and taste the world with. To the ever-smiling and accessible Jennifer Howard, who, with her quiet, peaceful, and unassuming but powerful talent, gave me the gift of writing flash fiction—no small task, indeed!

To my students, cohorts, colleagues, professors, friends and relatives from: Northern Michigan University, the city of Marquette, different parts of the United States, India, the United Kingdom and South Africa, thank you for your support, encouragement, feedback, collaboration and love through long evening walks by Lake Superior, wine drinking nights by the fire, be it by a chimenea, a log fire, or the fireplace in your homes and in your hearts, ice walks on the beach, long drives to waterfalls and lighthouses in the summer, fall color tours to near and far places in Michigan and Sault Ontario, long drives through meadows, kloofs, and galliyans of England, South Africa and India, respectively, swims in cold Superior in warm summer days and evenings, sunning on boulders by the shores, or simply sharing a meal and a drink at the Landmark Inn's Sky Room: I appreciate you. I thank you all from the bottom of my heart!

Thanks also goes to the Department of English at Northern Michigan University and to Finishing Line Press for believing in my writing and seeing enough beauty in my words to provide me an opportunity to share them with my readers.

I extend gratitude and love to Uzma Ahmed and Shravan Rajagopal for the cover painting of my mother and for providing help with the graphic art of the British India map, respectively.

Appreciation goes to the editors of journal where poems (and videopoems) in *Exiles and Pleasures: Taunggyi Dreaming* first appeared: *Superpresent, Hole in the Head Review, The Offbeat: Only to Reappear, The Offbeat: With Abandon, Harbor Review* and *South Asian Review*.

Jaspal Kaur Singh is a poet, writer, and an educator. She has a Ph.D. in Comparative Literature (University of Oregon) and a Master of Fine Arts (Northern Michigan University). Jaspal's book publications include: two monographs, *Violence and Resistance in Sikh Gendered Identity* (Routledge 2020) and *Representation and Resistance: Indian and African Women Writers at Home and in the Diaspora* (University of Calgary Press 2008); a coauthored book, *Narrating the New Nation: South African Indian Writing* (Peter Lang, 2018); coedited books, *Negotiating Gender and Sexuality in Contemporary Turkey* (Peter Lang, 2016), *Indian Writers: Transnationalisms and Diasporas* (Peter Lang, 2010), and *Trauma, Resistance, Reconciliation in Post-1994 South African Writing* (Peter Lang, 2010). Jaspal's poems and essays have appeared in *South Asian Review, The Offbeat, Dreadlocks Interrupted, Emergences: Journal for the Study of Media and Composite Cultures, In Other Words: An American Poetry Anthology, Philosophy and Global Affairs, Harbor Review,* among others. Jaspal has also created and published videopoems in *Superpresent: Magazine for the Arts* and *Hole in the Head Review*. She was born and raised in Burma, lived in India and Iraq, and migrated to the US in 1984 and, for now, calls Portland, Oregon home.

www.ingramcontent.com/pod-product-compliance
Lightning Source LLC
Chambersburg PA
CBHW030222170426
43194CB00007BA/832